Sliced Fruit and Other Love Languages

by Chelsea Hui
illustrated by Maria del Mar Mulet Picornell

Sliced Fruit and Other Love Languages copyright © 2022 by Chelsea Hui. All rights reserved. No part of this publication may be reproduced, distributed, or transmitted in any form or by any means without written permission except for the use of brief quotations in a book review.

ISBN: 978-0-9876340-4-7

To my mother -

for teaching me to how to love,
and be loved.

Trigger Warning:

The contents of this book contains references to racism, sexism and sexual assault.

In Chinese culture, love is not always expressed through fond words or an affectionate touch. For those who did not grow up in a bi-cultural household, our love may seem unfamiliar, at times, even distant. It does not boast or talk loudly but lives in the silences between unspoken words and the subtle acts of service that often go unnoticed and without thanks. To me, to my sister, and to the many children who grew up in immigrant households, love looks as simple as a bowl of perfectly cut fruit after dinner. It is a mother's selfless act of peeling and plucking all pits and skins, removing any hardness and leaving only the sweet softness of a piece of fruit. It is only ever eating the leftover flesh from the rind to keep the best parts for her children.

I wrote *Sliced Fruit and Other Love Languages* to speak to the friction and beauty of the Asian diaspora experience. Split into three lessons from childhood: *Love Is Tolerant, Love Is Strong, and Love is Kind*, the book grapples with the intricacies of affection, the trauma of generational and cultural dissonance, and the sacrifice of a mother's love. It tells the tale of how these formative experiences, seemingly big or small, manifest themselves in strange and sometimes even painful ways. This book speaks truth into my own journey, in hopes that telling one woman's story can help even one person feel less alone in theirs.

For every piece of fruit you ever cut for me, I hear the conversation between our hearts. The language your mother, and her mother, taught you to speak. The subtle gesture that you and I know means, *I love you.*

Part 1:
Love Is Tolerant

Where did you learn
to tolerate that which you should not accept,
to give away parts of yourself,
and settle for an existence,
far below what you were promised.

Generational Trauma

I'm working to lift the trauma that sits above my shoulders, one generation at a time. I am processing the tough love of childhood that has manifested itself in echoes of *not enough* or *too much*. I am untying the connection I have forged between my achievements and my self-worth. I am unlearning, and learning, so that my children, and theirs, will not have to.

Just Because It Is Familar, Does Not Mean It Is Love

You love the cold, because
you were born of it,
who taught you that love looks like this? relief
on the best of days, anxiety
on the worst,
who showed you that love thrives here,
beside self-doubt and insecurity,
who hurt you so much,
that you continued to hurt yourself,
even after they were gone.
who taught you that love,
should feel like self-harm?

Never Enough

I grew up believing I was never enough, and no matter how much time I spend in self-help books or inside the pages of a journal, somehow, I still believe that heaven is too far to reach. That it was not built for the demons that exist within me.

Black Opium

I wake as dawn breaks the night,
trickling through the gaps in your blinds,
to permeate this space
that smells so much of sleep
and my perfume,
I wake
and your eyes smile at me,

and I love you,
and I try to empty my mind of the thought
that I would give up
everything good that I have,
to see you happy.

The Mystery of The Orient

We read the stories,
and believed every word –

Women who look like us,
are weak for men who look like him,
a *mystery of the orient,*
new, unchartered territory,
waiting to be conquered.

we watched our identities fall into falsehood,
that our skin would never be seen for what it was,
as anything more than exotic,

alien,

other.

Chelsea Hui

Eggshells

You wear your empathy and your tolerance,
like a badge of honour,
rather than a mark of trauma,
a hidden tragedy,
that somewhere a little girl had to learn to survive,
by reading and re-reading the emotions,
of the adults around her.

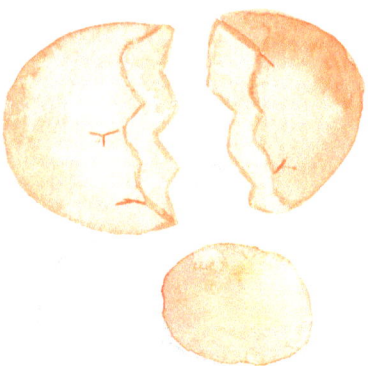

Whatever It Takes

The way I treat my body
reminds me of the human urge to capture,
to preserve beautiful things
even if it means killing it.

Tides and Tears

The moon,
she cries for you,
she feels every droplet,
every tear,
as she pulls water from tide to tide,
she knows your pain,
and she cries with you.

'This is not love.'

one of the hardest truths I had to admit

I was never enough for him.

no...
she said,
you are the one you weren't enough for.

- a conversation with my therapist

Chelsea Hui

You're Pretty For An Asian Girl

You tell me that I'm beautiful for my kind,
that despite my culture
and the burden that it carries,
I am still desirable,
as if I would somehow be grateful,
that you deemed me acceptable,
more worthy than my sisters.

Toxic Love

I cannot believe how long I convinced myself,
that fear is what love should look like.

Chelsea Hui

*I am who has loved me,
Who has hurt me.*

Half A Lover

I am a porcelain bowl:
shattered remnants of my psyche
pieced together
with the glue of a million lovers,
hiding the cracks,
the scars I put there myself.

Every so often,
when a piece of me unravels
and the bond bears to break,
I face the reality
that my heart is not yet full enough
to hold myself.

It Will Pass

You won't feel this way forever.

You won't feel this way forever.

You won't feel this way forever.

You can't.

Do I Even Want To Heal?

What does it mean to forgive,
if the word merely hangs off my tongue,
in the hopes of saving what was,
I hold onto the fabric of it,
of what you did,
to me,
to us,
ringing it in my hands until they're numb,
because in some twisted way,
the pain is my only hope
that anything has changed.

Chelsea Hui

How Do You Sleep At Night?

I wonder if you stay up
hating yourself for what you did,
As much as I lie awake
hating myself for forgiving you.

Chelsea Hui

Break Your Heart Apart

How many times
did you have to break
your chest open,
for him
to finally see
your heart hurting?

I'm Sorry, No One's Home

I constructed an existence,
within the rules they made,
wrote a story,
they told me the world wanted to read,

I crafted a woman,
they deemed worthy of love,
yet still,
it is lonely here,

in the end,
when I come home to myself,
and look around at the life I have built,
I see,
that I am the only one who lives here.

Emotional Scars

Sometimes you can still feel a bruise,
long after it has already healed.

Yellow Fever

I took the self-loathing
and resentment for my skin,
I buried it inside men who did not deserve me,
searching for validation, belonging
in a sea of backhanded compliments,
yellow fever masqueraded as attraction,
trying to find a home,
in the same people
who told my ancestors to go back to theirs.

Chelsea Hui

I want to apologise
to the women I have undermined,
for fear
that the space they took up
would, somehow, shrink my own.

- the lies we are taught to tell our daughters

One-Sided Affairs

I held his heart between my hands,
not knowing if I'd ever loved anything more,
or how to let it go.

I cradled it for as long as my palms would allow,
until the day,
he asked for it back.

Same Shade of Blue

I cannot fix you,
and you cannot save me.

Now I see,
it was silly of us to even try,
just because our hearts beat
the same pace,
just because we cry
the same shade of blue.

Bottled Up

Fostering communities that refuse to talk,
Create generations of youth
who are all collectively alone.

Fair Trade

I traded my reality
for a fantasy.

I gave up my truth
for a promise.

I lost myself
to find you,
I've been searching
for a way back ever since.

Shore

I want to rip your name from her lips
and throw it back into the ocean,
along the skirts of the sand
where the water kisses the shoreline
like you used to kiss me,
before you let the tide wash it all away,
all my trust,
all our love,
leaving behind only an imprint,
memories that are already fading day by day.

Chelsea Hui

I want to know who you think of:
who is it that you miss,
when you read my words?

Free From You

I tear off my clothes
and throw them in the hamper across the room.

I start to scrub my body clean of you,
didn't you deserve it?

I feel numb,
as the foam washes over my stomach,
down my legs,
swirling towards the drain,
didn't you ask for it?

I sit,
drenched in the corner,
watching as the water carries you
away from me,
washing your sins clean off my skin.

False Fantasies

He dangled the promise of better,
inches above her head,
close enough to want,
but too far to ever have.

Love Is Blind

I made a deal with the devil,
thinking he was cupid.

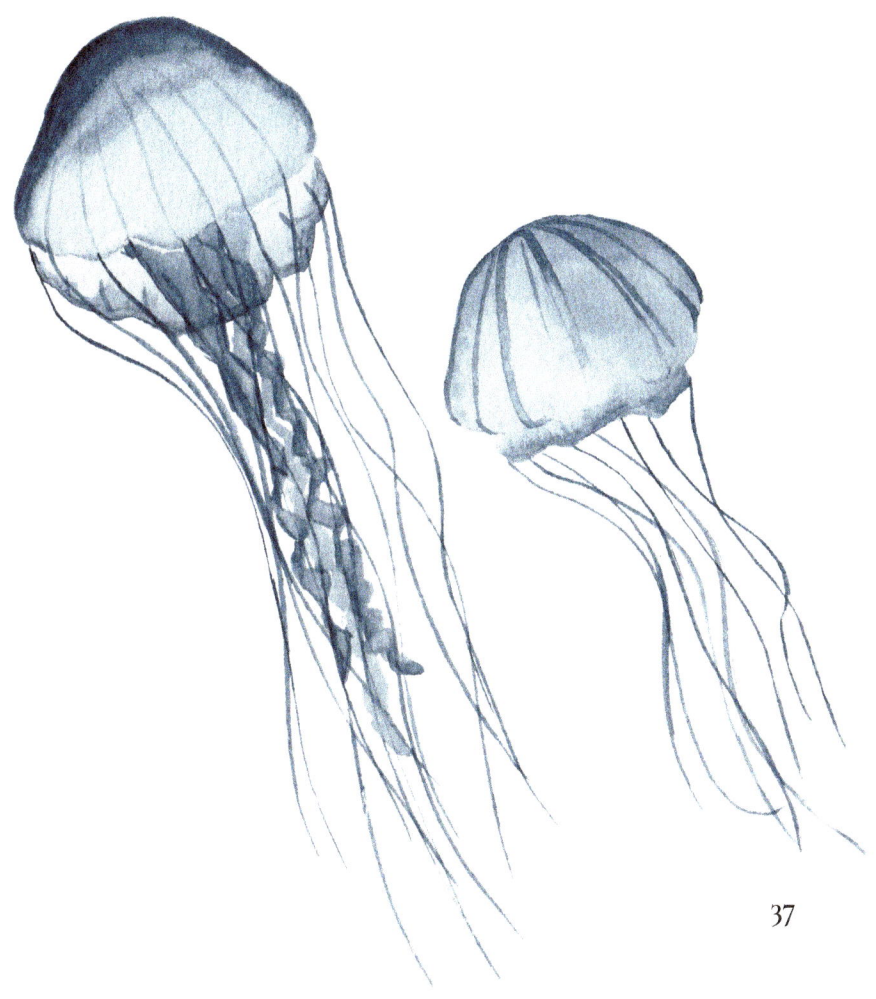

Chelsea Hui

Why Do You Love Those Who Hurt You?

He loves me,
he loves me not,

How many more petals will you pluck from yourself,
for someone who is unsure of your beauty.

Loneliness

This time,
The silence might actually kill me.

Inferior

It is never enough:
no amount of lovers,
intimacy, success
or achievement,
have ever been enough,
none of it
will do what you want,
to fill the insatiable need,
to be understood,
to be seen,
to be loved,
for simply being
just as you are.

Are we all unconsciously,
And consciously,
repeating past mistakes,
refusing to move forward
just to complete patterns of old.

- learned behaviours

Part 2: Love Is Strong

Your trauma has given you
empathy,
compassion,
perspective,
it has given you the strength to continue.

Mama

You gave
so that we could receive,

you knew sacrifice
so we would not have to.

You wore down your world,
to build ours up,

I am,
because you did,

and no matter how much time passes,
I will not forget:

一千年
a thousand years,

一萬年
ten thousand years,

我會愛你
I will love you.

Chelsea Hui

I constantly find myself
being stuck
between coping and healing.

Timing

I finally chose to forgive you and myself,
for outgrowing the promises we made as young lovers.

Feminine Power

You should know that you are infinite,
that you are magic,
that you have it all.

You should know that your femininity
is your strength,
not your downfall.

My Girl

I belong wholly to myself, and I
worship at the feet of my own altar,
every damn day
I meditate to the sound of my thoughts,
my dreams, my energy
and each morning I pray to myself,
a reminder of my worth,
until it is etched into my soul,
and reverberated through my being,
that I am whole, I am enough
and I belong to no one.

Sometimes Asking For Help Is The Greatest Act of Courage

Somehow, I feel ashamed to admit
that sometimes,
I need you
to numb the bite,
to pull the pain from my heart,
the weight that sits above my shoulders,
to hold me,
to get me
through the hard part of the night.

Inner Child

I'm still waiting
to meet my purest self,
to find the girl I left behind,
and tell her I love her.

Pussy Power

From the force between my thighs,
flows pain, pleasure, power,
I can think of nothing more fearless
than this temple of life
and desire,
birthing stories of love
and survival.

Entitlement Is Not Sexy

Persistence after resistance,
is not romance –

these are the lessons
we must reteach
our children.

Chelsea Hui

To Love And Be Loved...

Find the ones who follow your light where it travels.
who go with you to the places where you love,
and feel loved.

Period Cramps

Each new moon brings with it
the ache of a new possibility,
it washes over her senses,
flows through her uterus,
grasping her body
with an excruciating hold,
just as her mother,
and her mother did,
she coexists with the pain,
and rises again,
with each new moon.

For My Father's Father

Forgive me
for my ancestors,
for the generations of sacrifice
that have been met with the hate
you so freely give.

Forgive me
for the inconvenience of my survival,
for the measures I will take
to protect my culture,
and my people.

Forgive me,
Forgive me,
for I have the audacity
to demand my own equality.

Sacrifice

I feel guilt for the dreams lost,
or the ones never uncovered,
because of the sacrifice she made
for me,
and you.

I often wonder,
how much she didn't do for herself,
to do it all for us,
how much of her soul she gave away,
to make ours feel full.

Chelsea Hui

To The Women Who Came Before Me

I owe it to the shoulders that have carried me,
to the foundations on which I stand,
from where I reach new heights,
from which I strive,
from which we vanquish,

together.

Resilience

There is pain and comfort in knowing, you can
break a million times, and still
piece yourself back together
just once more.

Shared Burdens

What it must feel like
to walk with an entire community on your back,
as if one wrong move,
would topple the progress of a thousand generations.

Broken English

I listen for the gaps in a sentence,
prolonged pauses,
26 letters running through her mind
all at once,
slurred between her diction,
I listen and I hear her strength,
I hear the life they sought for their children,
punctuated with fragments of the life, the familiarity
they had to leave behind,

I listen,

I listen,
and all I can hear
is the sound of her heart.

Self Acceptance

It is both a gift and a curse,
to be a woman of two worlds,
born of two cultures,
bred in two places.

When I am homesick for one,
I find solace in another,
but too often, I feel like one,
and not enough like the other.

It is both a gift and a curse,
to be in a constant state of conflict
with one's identity.

Chelsea Hui

There Is Life After

In the end,
it was not the tragedy
you thought it would be,
you did not break as brutally,
fall quite as far,
as you were scared you might,

in the end,
it was not the end at all.

Moonlight

Do you still talk to the moon,
like you once spoke to me?

Do you tell her of your worries,
and your dreams?

Do you speak to her as if her ear,
is the mantle from which reality is born,
as if her understanding speaks truth?

Anything is possible,
the future is boundless,
because her belief
is the only promise you needed,
to take your first step
into the unknown.

Hard Nights

Most mornings I watch
the sun fight her way over the horizon
and seep under the crack of my door,
she wraps her soft rays around me,
as if to tell me it's okay now,
as if she knows
what the hours before her carried.

She knows,
that at night,
when the chatter stops
and I finally lay down,
is when the heart aches the most.

Chelsea Hui

I know you're aching,
but – remember - that to feel
hurt is to be alive.

Chelsea Hui

My City, My Fire

I was born of fire,
those flames given to me by the very city
from which my elders came from,
under a horizon that never sleeps
and a people that never fade,
her heart beats with a desire,
a strength to continue,
to persevere
against all that keeps her down.

I am a product of a culture,
of resilience,
of freedom,
of an immortal legacy.

Shame

I want you to know,
that the woman you saw,
the woman you knew:
she doesn't live here anymore
and self-hatred
no longer lives in this body
and guilt,
no longer
plagues this mind.

She is free
to discover
and to love,
to exist in her skin,
without the shame
you left inside her.

Enough Is Enough

That lie
was the only thing I needed,
to kill off the man I thought I had,
to mourn the future you'd promised me,
to say goodbye
to the woman who once loved you.

Face Yourself

I have spent enough of my youth running from my own reflection to know,
that no matter how many times you turn away from the mirror,
you will still have to face your heart,
and your soul,
at the end of each day.

Chelsea Hui

Woman,
means *human*.

Muse

My poetry speaks of my existence,
these lines
a contour of my figure,
my words
a translation of these lips,
all these stories through my eyes,
I am my own muse.

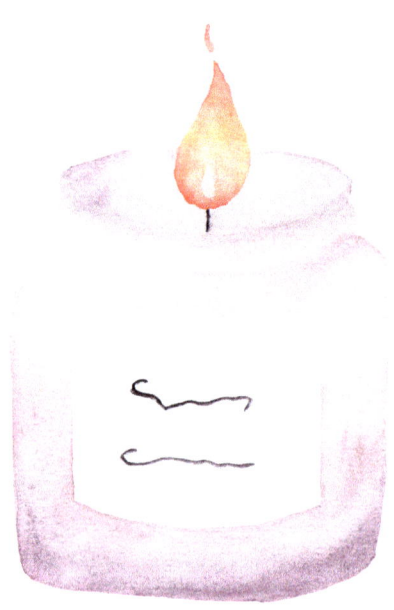

Metamorphosis

With every blessing the universe gives, every
opportunity it takes,
I am changing,
and blooming,

I am rising.

Chelsea Hui

If you knew her story, perhaps
you would not judge her so harshly.

Colourblindness Is Erasure

Women of colour, we see you,
we know you,
we honour you.

Mothering

She chose motherhood and it was the most selfless, thankless job she would ever have. I once asked her if she ever regretted it. Admist all the other possibilities and paths, she told me that, whether it was this lifetime, or the next, or the lifetime after that, she would choose us

over and over again.

Chelsea Hui

True love never gives up,

and yet,
I love myself enough
to walk away from any situation,
that has given up on my happiness.

Growing Pains

Unlearning the lessons they taught us,
is not disrespect to our mothers and fathers,
it is the ultimate respect
to yourself and your peace,

give yourself permission to heal.

Part 3:
Love Is Kind

To truly be in love,
is to approach softly,
to handle others,
and even your own heart,
with care.

Love Is Soft. Love Is Sweet.

From my mother and her mother,
I learnt that love tastes sweet and soft,
a bowl of carefully-cut fruit after dinner,
where all the pits, seeds,
and all the hardness,
have already been removed,
leaving only the best parts for me.

It's in the way she carefully carves away the rind,
saving only the flesh around the pit for herself,
sucking on the skin as to not let it go to waste,
that is the love I grew up with,
that, to me, is love
more than words could convey,
that, to me, is love
of the greatest sacrifice.

Chelsea Hui

Why I Read

I live and I love amongst the lyrics,
the poems,
the words,
I couldn't find within myself.

Stay Soft

Today, I hope you choose softness –
I hope kindness finds you amidst the cruelty and the hurt.

That it holds your hand amongst the ruin.

If I don't get the chance to tell you -
I really loved you.

Nature's Heart

In her heart grew a sanctuary of love,
A place where new life sprouted from old tears
and lessons learned,
A garden of contentment,
A place she enjoyed all to herself.

The Truth About Moving On

The truth is:
I think about that day a lot. More than I probably should.
And though we've crossed paths before, this time I really hope
you know that I meant it.

I meant it when I asked how you'd been. I meant it when I said
I hoped you were happy. And I meant it when I let you embrace me
like you once did, an attempt to translate the words my lips could not
possibly utter to you, anymore.

Because the truth is:
I have moved on and I miss you.

The truth is:
I am happy and I miss you.

And only 4 years later, have I come to understand how
you can love someone from afar. How you can love someone
and still move on without them.

One Day... It Will Make Sense

When we look back,
we'll see
we were both better
because of it.

The Window To My Soul

My love language lives in the man
who does not read, but has consumed
every word I have ever written, to feel closer
to my soul.

Purple

I cannot see the colour
purple
without picturing that lilac sky,
the bleeding clouds,
your dark silhouette,
the chill of the night's breath
against our warm cheeks,
I cannot see the colour
purple,
without thinking of you,
and that typical Thursday night.

Twin Flames

If there is a God,
she must love me the most,
when she separated our souls,
she sent you to mother first,

I know she did that for me,
for my fragile heart,
so that the second I arrived,
you would be waiting.

Waiting to show me the way,
before I even knew how to walk,
and to hold my hand
at times I could not hold myself.

I will not take her kindness for granted,
nor can I ever return yours,
but I will be forever chasing you,
following in your footsteps,

until the day our souls meet again.

Chelsea Hui

Love that is safe,

Love that keeps promises,

Love that feels like home.

Love Stories

I make poetry out of our lives,
so that years later,
long after the dust has settled,
our love story will still exist
somewhere.

Under The Stars

That night,
under the stars,
I didn't tell you,
but my heart ached,
not because of anything in particular,
just a thought,
the thought that,
how,
amidst all the chaos,
and noise,
we found a moment like this.

Chelsea Hui

we are creatures that live
and love only a short while,

so let us.

You Are Enough

My story is not finished,
yet I am complete,
I am whole already.

Chelsea Hui

Mosaic

Since you've left, I've been trying
to pick up the pieces,
and what, at first, seemed broken,
now looks only scarred,
the cuts from past trauma,
past memories, are not shards
of a broken person,
but fragments of a life,
making up a colourful, intricate mosaic,
an artwork through time,
comprised of experiences,
lessons, for my trauma
has not broken me,
it has made me.

If Hearts Did Not Break

If everyone was as gentle with others,
as loving,
as you are,
I fear songwriters
and great poets,
would have nothing left to write about.

Family Traditions

The crack of a can,
a sizzling pop
as my mother pours coke into a glass,
We had this only twice a year,
a treat when I was young, my father says.

Around us,
the halls,
the doors dressed in red,
and the air chimes of a fresh start,
I bring the chilled glass to my lips,
and I taste nostalgia,
a tradition to remind us of all that we have,
to never take something so seemingly small,
for granted.

Chelsea Hui

11:11

At least twice a day,
I know you
will be thinking of me.

Women

The women in my life are magic,
conjuring from me enigmas
and truths,
I had not yet understood myself.

Chelsea Hui

Love looks good on you,
When you are not craving it through another's eyes.

Chelsea Hui

Speak Softly

Your words hold more weight,
cut deeper than you know,
learn to speak softly and hold your heart,
as you would another's.

God Is A Woman Who Loves Me

She breathes life,
like the mother who raised me,
with hands gentle yet worn,
from holding her own world.

She blooms love
in the flowers that grow by the river,
and in the children that will grow
to remake a broken world.

She hears you,
she sees you,
God is a woman who loves you,
and she exists all around us.

Growth

Do you ever give yourself credit
for learning to sprout flowers,
from the dirt left behind
by memories that almost buried you?

Chelsea Hui

Mother Nature, herself.

Love surrounds her
because she was born of it,
just as it is created through her,
an ecosystem of tenderness
that exists all within her belly,
sprouting life
like mother nature herself,
she is the reason,
that we know,
that we leave this world
the same way
we came into it:

with love.

Chelsea Hui

You are only as pretty as you are kind.

- my mother's greatest lesson to me.

Hopelessly In Love

I am learning to romanticise
every detail of every
minute, of every day.

I am learning to love
the smallest details
in the smallest ways.

I am learning to love life
as it is, and not
as I hope it to be.

Unlikely Friendships

Not just friends,
never quite lovers,
yet the best of friends,
quite unknowingly in love,
caught in conversations
that ate up the night,
you send poems to me,
for me, about me,
you read my words,
and I proof yours,
drunk texts,
3 months,
then 6 months,
now years apart
and to this day,
I think of you and I smile,
I think of you and I feel giddy,
that I once met a boy,
who knew how to solve my mind's intellectual maze,
as easy as if it were a reflection of his own.

Kindness

The harshness you give cannot break me,
the softness is melded in my bones,
the kindness lives in my veins,
a gift from my mother,
the very day I was born.

Lullaby

Waking up with you,
I realised I had slept
through the night
for the first time in weeks,

How profound it is,
to be able to spend my days
with the one who makes the nights
feel so much shorter.

To The Man Who Loves Me

To the man who taught me strength, who
may not have always known how to hold my hand,
but would always walk not even one step behind me,
just so I would know he was there. To the man
who raised two girls to believe that this world was built for them,
in a world he knew was not. To the man who shies away
from opening his heart
but would give his daughters every last piece of it,
if they needed it.

To the man who was never shown softness
or taught the importance of kindness,
but is learning every day.

To the man who loves me in the ways that he knows.

Chelsea Hui

In Case You Forget, Mama

When you look back on your life,
I want you to know,
I want you to remember,
that you are the reason I believe
in kindness, in goodness,
and why I carry it with me
every step of the way.

Why Do You Write?

The art we make is simply a conversation with the children we once were.

Acknowledgements:

First of all, thank *you*. My readers. Whether you have been supporting me since before *Yellow* was published or if this is the first time you have read my words, I want to thank you from the bottom of my heart. Being a self-published poet is no easy journey, so if you have chosen to use your hard earned money to purchase one of my books, if you have ever sent me an encouraging message, reposted one of my poems, or shared my work, I want to express my eternal gratitude to you. Thank you for giving me a reason to continue.

A sincere, heartfelt thank you to my artist and collaborator, Maria. Thank you for pouring your heart onto these pages in order to help me express what is in mine. This is our triumph.

Thank you to my family:

To my person, Vishan. Together we have learnt the beauty, the discomfort, and the necessity of growth. I have met few men who are as resilient, self-reflexive, and vulnerable as you. Thank you for always holding me and inspiring me to do better everyday.

To my big sister, Janice. To feel completely and entirely understood by another person is a gift few people get to experience. I am so lucky to have found my soulmate in you. Thank you for protecting me, seeing me, and loving me.

To my father. So many things we desired in this life have been made possible because of you and your love for your daughters. Thank you for carrying me on your shoulders so that I could reach for the stars.

And lastly, to my mother. The woman who inspired this collection and my life. No words can ever truly hold all that you mean to me and all that I owe you. This book is my reminder to you that your love, your kindness, your sacrifice do not go unnoticed. You are the reason I am who I am. I love you.

Find Chelsea here

🌐 chelseahui.com

📷 @_chelseahui

📷 @huimusings

Find Maria here

📷 @seamlybymar

CPSIA information can be obtained
at www.ICGtesting.com
Printed in the USA
LVHW020137211122
733501LV00003B/118